Collins

easy learning

Times tables

Ages 5–7

3 ×2 24

Simon Greaves
Helen Greaves

How to use this book

- Find a quiet, comfortable place to work, away from other distractions.
- Help with reading the instructions where necessary and ensure that your child understands what they are required to do.
- Help and encourage your child to check their own answers as they complete each activity.
- Discuss with your child what they have learnt.
- Let your child return to their favourite pages once they have been completed, to talk about the activities.
- Reward your child with plenty of praise and encouragement.

Special features

- Yellow boxes: Introduce and outline the key times tables ideas.
- Did you know …? boxes: Give handy hints to help understanding of the key times tables ideas.

The author and publisher are grateful to the copyright holders for permission to use quoted materials and images.

Cover: © Klara Viskova / Shutterstock.com
p6, 9, 13, 17: © Asaf Eliason / Shutterstock.com

Published by Collins
An imprint of HarperCollinsPublishers
1 London Bridge Street
London SE1 9GF

Browse the complete Collins catalogue at www.collins.co.uk

© HarperCollinsPublishers 2011
This edition © HarperCollinsPublishers 2015

10 9 8 7 6 5 4 3 2

ISBN-13 978-0-00-813438-9

The author asserts his moral right to be identified as the author of this work.

British Library Cataloguing in Publication Data

A Catalogue record for this publication is available from the British Library

Written by Simon Greaves and Helen Greaves
Design and layout by G Brasnett, Cambridge and Jouve
Illustrated by Jenny Tulip
Cover design by Sarah Duxbury and Paul Oates
Project managed by Sonia Sawkins

Contents

Two times table

Read the two times table out loud.

1 × 2 = 2

2 × 2 = 4

3 × 2 = 6

4 × 2 = 8

5 × 2 = 10

6 × 2 = 12

7 × 2 = 14

8 × 2 = 16

9 × 2 = 18

10 × 2 = 20

11 × 2 = 22

12 × 2 = 24

Now fill in these answers.

2 × ☐ = 2

☐ × 2 = 4

2 × 3 = ☐

2 × ☐ = 8

☐ × 5 = 10

2 × 6 = ☐

2 × 7 = ☐

☐ × 8 = 16

2 × ☐ = 18

2 × ☐ = 20

2 × ☐ = 22

2 × 12 = ☐

Did you know ... ?

All the answers in the two times table are **even** numbers.

An even number ends in **0**, **2**, **4**, **6**, or **8**.

1 The frog wants to get the fly. Colour the path only using the answers in the two times table.

13 1 9 8

19 3 16

5

2 20 23 24 11

10 7 14 18

22

15 12

2 Every number put into the number machine is **doubled**. Doubled means multiplied by **2**.

Fill in the missing numbers.

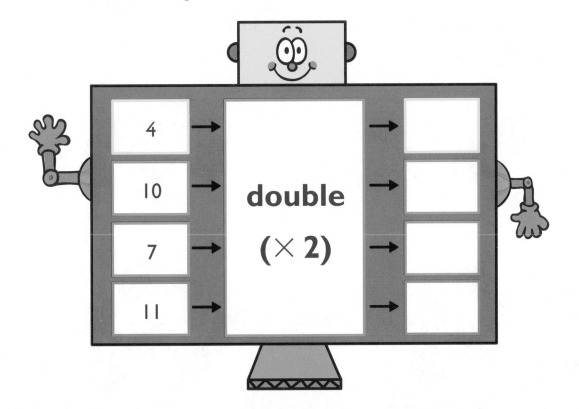

4 → double (× 2) →

10 →

7 →

11 →

3 Count the coins and complete each multiplication.

$2 \times \boxed{2} \text{ p} = \boxed{4} \text{ p}$

$\boxed{} \times \boxed{2} \text{ p} = \boxed{20} \text{ p}$

$\boxed{} \times \boxed{2} \text{ p} = \boxed{} \text{ p}$

$\boxed{} \times \boxed{} \text{ p} = \boxed{} \text{ p}$

$\boxed{} \times \boxed{} \text{ p} = \boxed{} \text{ p}$

4 Socks come in pairs. There are two socks in each pair.

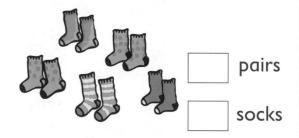

$\boxed{1}$ pair
$\boxed{2}$ socks

For each picture write the number of pairs and socks.

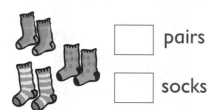

$\boxed{}$ pairs
$\boxed{}$ socks

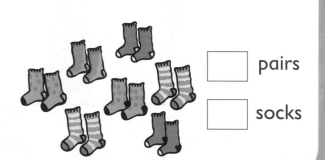

$\boxed{}$ pairs
$\boxed{}$ socks

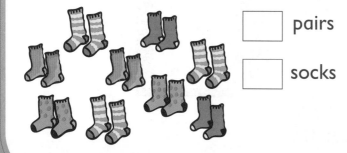

$\boxed{}$ pairs
$\boxed{}$ socks

$\boxed{}$ pairs
$\boxed{}$ socks

5 Draw a line to join each child to their matching kite.

6 If you roll two dice together you can get six different 'doubles'. You could get 1 and 1. This double scores 2.

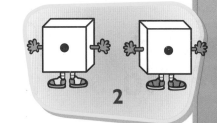

Draw dots on the dice to show doubles with these total scores.

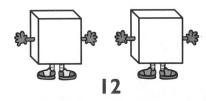
8

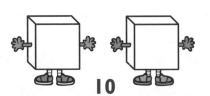
4

6

10

12

Ten times table

Read the ten times table out loud.

$1 \times 10 = 10$

$2 \times 10 = 20$

$3 \times 10 = 30$

$4 \times 10 = 40$

$5 \times 10 = 50$

$6 \times 10 = 60$

$7 \times 10 = 70$

$8 \times 10 = 80$

$9 \times 10 = 90$

$10 \times 10 = 100$

$11 \times 10 = 110$

$12 \times 10 = 120$

Now fill in these answers.

$10 \times \boxed{} = 10$

$\boxed{} \times 2 = 20$

$10 \times 3 = \boxed{}$

$\boxed{} \times 4 = 40$

$10 \times 5 = \boxed{}$

$10 \times \boxed{} = 60$

$\boxed{} \times 7 = 70$

$10 \times \boxed{} = 80$

$10 \times 9 = \boxed{}$

$\boxed{} \times 10 = 100$

$10 \times \boxed{} = 110$

$10 \times 12 = \boxed{}$

Did you know ... ?

All the answers in the ten times table **end in zero**.

10, 20, 30, 40, 50, 60, 70, 80, 90, 100, 110, 120

1 Write a multiplication to show the total amount of money.

| 3 | × | 10 | p | = | 30 | p |

| | × | 10 | p | = | | p |

| | × | | p | = | | p |

| | × | | p | = | | p |

2 Colour green all the shapes that have an answer in the ten times table.

What do you see?

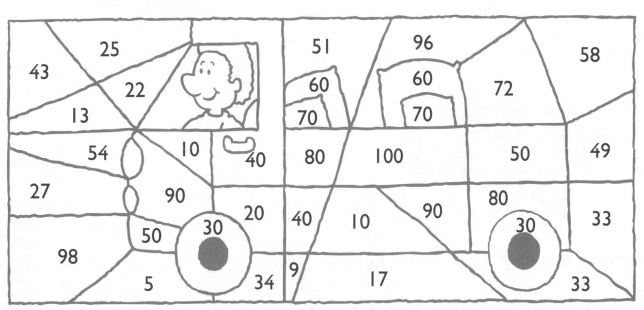

3 Here is some fruit for sale.

9p   8p   5p   7p   11p

How much will it cost to buy:

10 pears [ ]p   10 oranges [ ]p   10 peaches [ ]p

10 bananas [ ]p   10 apples [ ]p

4 Write a multiplication to show the number of fingers on the pairs of gloves in each group.

| 2 | × | 10 | = | 20 |

[ ] × [ ] = [ ]

[ ] × [ ] = [ ]

[ ] × [ ] = [ ]

How many fingers on twelve pairs of gloves? [ ]

There are ninety fingers. How many pairs of gloves are there? [ ]

5 Every number put into the number machine is multiplied by 10.

Fill in the missing numbers.

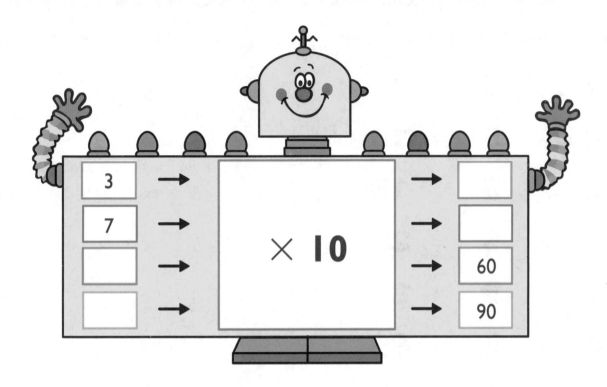

6 Say the multiples of ten as you join the dots. Join them in order.

What do you see?

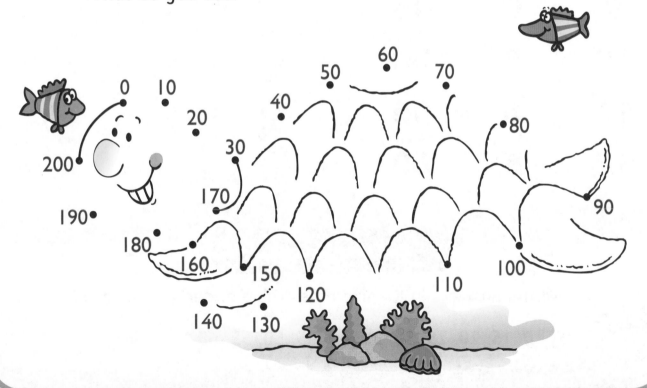

Five times table

Read the five times table out loud.

1 × 5 = 5

2 × 5 = 10

3 × 5 = 15

4 × 5 = 20

5 × 5 = 25

6 × 5 = 30

7 × 5 = 35

8 × 5 = 40

9 × 5 = 45

10 × 5 = 50

11 × 5 = 55

12 × 5 = 60

Now fill in these answers.

☐ × 1 = 5

5 × 2 = ☐

5 × ☐ = 15

5 × 4 = ☐

5 × ☐ = 25

☐ × 6 = 30

5 × 7 = ☐

5 × 8 = ☐

☐ × 9 = 45

5 × ☐ = 50

5 × ☐ = 55

☐ × 12 = 60

Did you know ... ?

All the answers in the five times table end in **five** or **zero**.

5, 10, 15, 20, 25, 30, 35, 40, 45, 50, 55, 60

1 Complete these multiplications.

$$45 = \boxed{9} \times 5$$

$$30 = \bigcirc \times 5 \qquad 5 = \bigcirc \times 5 \qquad 20 = \bigcirc \times 5$$

$$50 = \bigcirc \times 5 \qquad 35 = \bigcirc \times 5 \qquad 10 = \bigcirc \times 5$$

$$15 = \bigcirc \times 5 \qquad 25 = \bigcirc \times 5 \qquad 60 = \bigcirc \times 5$$

2 Find the total in each purse.

$$\boxed{2} \times \boxed{5} \text{ p} = \boxed{10} \text{ p}$$

$$\boxed{} \times \boxed{5} \text{ p} = \boxed{} \text{ p}$$

$$\boxed{} \times \boxed{} \text{ p} = \boxed{} \text{ p}$$

$$\boxed{} \times \boxed{} \text{ p} = \boxed{} \text{ p}$$

Draw 5p pieces to show the amount next to each purse.

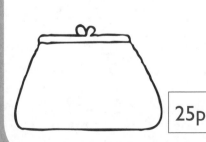 25p

 35p

40p

3 Help the rabbit get the carrots. Fill in the missing numbers on the path.

After 50, count on in fives to 100.

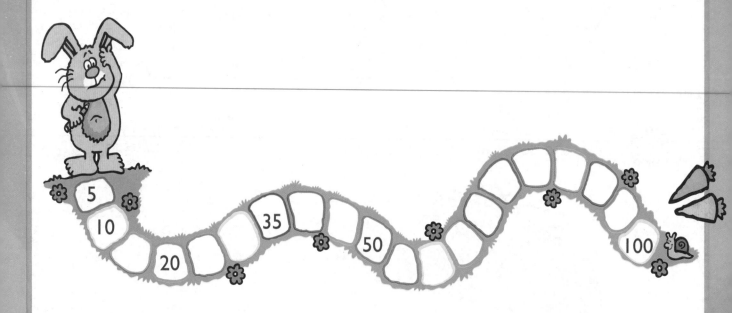

4 The cat can only catch fish which are answers in the five times table.

Colour the fish he can catch.

5 In each line, circle the multiplication that totals the number in the star.

35   7 × 5   6 × 5   8 × 5   5 × 5

50   4 × 5   8 × 5   10 × 5   6 × 5

10   5 × 5   1 × 5   10 × 5   2 × 5

55   2 × 5   11 × 5   10 × 5   5 × 5

6 Work out the answer to each multiplication. Then use the answer to find the correct colour in the code key.

Colour the picture.

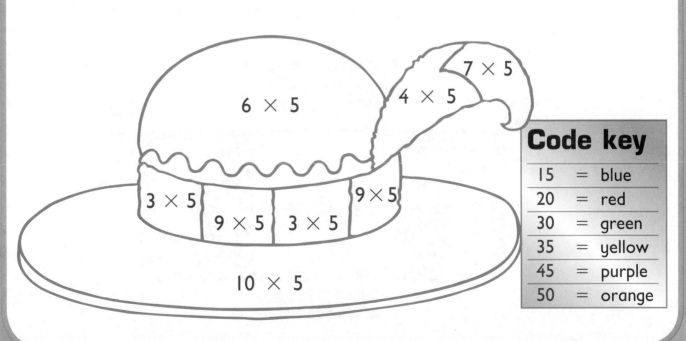

Code key		
15	=	blue
20	=	red
30	=	green
35	=	yellow
45	=	purple
50	=	orange

Mixed tables

1 Use the number machine to **double** each number.

Use the number machine to **halve** each number.

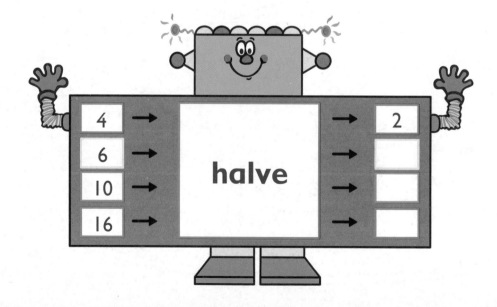

2 10p can be made using 2p, 5p or 10p coins.

Make 20p in each purse using 2p coins or 5p coins or 10p coins.

Draw the coins in the purse and write
the multiplication in the box below.

| | × 2p = | | p | | × 5p = | | p | | × 10p = | | p |

3 Work out the answer to each multiplication.
Then use the answer to find the correct
colour in the code key.

Colour the picture.

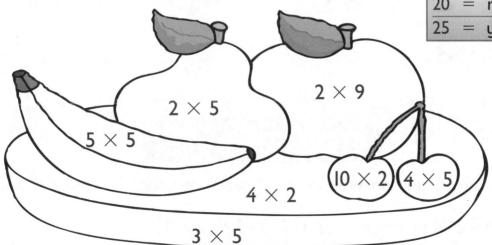

2 × 9

2 × 5

5 × 5

10 × 2   4 × 5

4 × 2

3 × 5

Three times table

Read the three times table out loud.

1	×	3	=	3
2	×	3	=	6
3	×	3	=	9
4	×	3	=	12
5	×	3	=	15
6	×	3	=	18
7	×	3	=	21
8	×	3	=	24
9	×	3	=	27
10	×	3	=	30
11	×	3	=	33
12	×	3	=	36

Now fill in these answers.

☐	×	1	=	3
3	×	☐	=	6
3	×	3	=	☐
3	×	☐	=	12
3	×	5	=	☐
☐	×	6	=	18
3	×	☐	=	21
3	×	8	=	☐
☐	×	9	=	27
3	×	☐	=	30
☐	×	11	=	33
3	×	12	=	☐

Did you know ... ?

Every other answer in the three times table is an **odd** number.

An odd number ends in **1**, **3**, **5**, **7**, or **9**.

18

1 A tricycle has three wheels.

Write a multiplication to show the number of wheels on the tricycles.

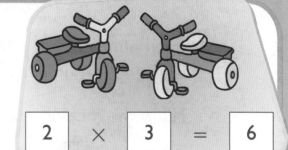

| 2 | × | 3 | = | 6 |

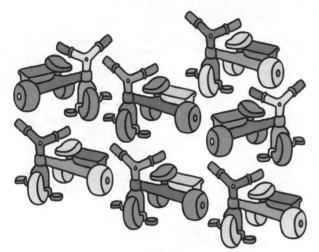

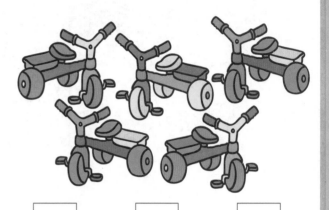

| | × | 3 | = | |

| | × | | = | |

| | × | | = | |

| | × | | = | |

2 Colour a path through the number grid.

Only go through answers to the three times table.

5	17	23	24	6	18	→ Finish
1	10	36	21	26	16	
2	20	15	29	28	11	
12	27	3	7	4	8	
Start → 9	22	13	14	19	25	

3 Each number that goes into the machine is multiplied by three.

Fill in the missing numbers.

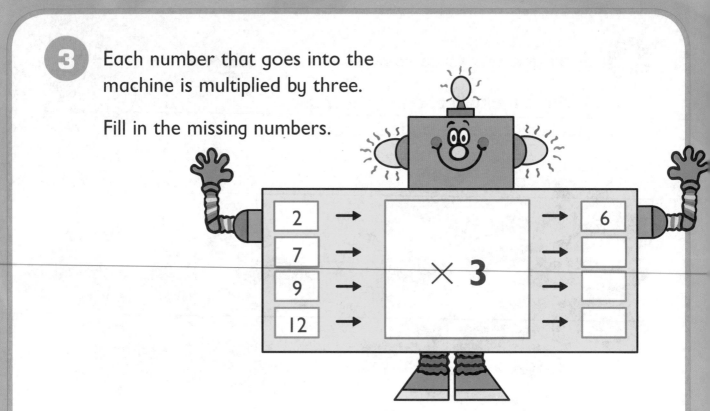

4 Colour each group of three sweets in a different colour.

Write a multiplication to show the number of sweets in each pile.

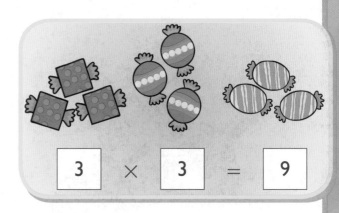

$$3 \times 3 = 9$$

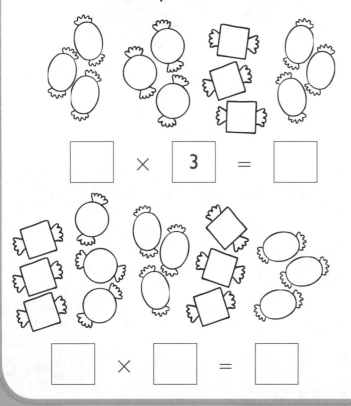

$$\boxed{} \times \boxed{3} = \boxed{}$$

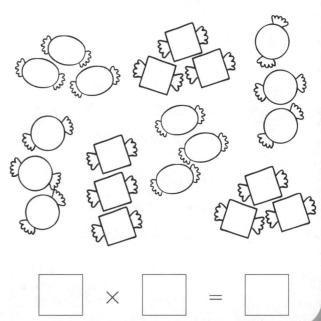

$$\boxed{} \times \boxed{} = \boxed{}$$

$$\boxed{} \times \boxed{} = \boxed{}$$

5 These toys are for sale.

How much would it cost to buy:

3 yo-yos ☐ p   3 crayons ☐ p   3 bears ☐ p

3 pencil sharpeners ☐ p   3 trains ☐ p

A pencil costs 3p.

How much would it cost to buy:

5 pencils ☐ p   7 pencils ☐ p   10 pencils ☐ p

6 Complete these multiplications using the three times table.

△ × 3 = 18   △ × 3 = 24

△ × 3 = 12   △ × 3 = 36

△ × 3 = 27   △ × 3 = 30

△ × 3 = 6   △ × 3 = 3

△ × 3 = 33   △ × 3 = 15

△ × 3 = 9   △ × 3 = 21

Four times table

Read the four times table out loud.

$1 \times 4 = 4$

$2 \times 4 = 8$

$3 \times 4 = 12$

$4 \times 4 = 16$

$5 \times 4 = 20$

$6 \times 4 = 24$

$7 \times 4 = 28$

$8 \times 4 = 32$

$9 \times 4 = 36$

$10 \times 4 = 40$

$11 \times 4 = 44$

$12 \times 4 = 48$

Now fill in these answers.

$4 \times \boxed{} = 4$

$4 \times 2 = \boxed{}$

$\boxed{} \times 3 = 12$

$4 \times 4 = \boxed{}$

$\boxed{} \times 5 = 20$

$4 \times \boxed{} = 24$

$4 \times 7 = \boxed{}$

$4 \times 8 = \boxed{}$

$\boxed{} \times 9 = 36$

$4 \times 10 = \boxed{}$

$4 \times \boxed{} = 44$

$\boxed{} \times 12 = 48$

Did you know ... ?

Words linked to the number four have the letter 'qua' in them.

Like **square** and **quarter**!

1 There are four cakes in a box.

Write a multiplication to show the number of cakes altogether.

$$2 \times 4 = 8$$

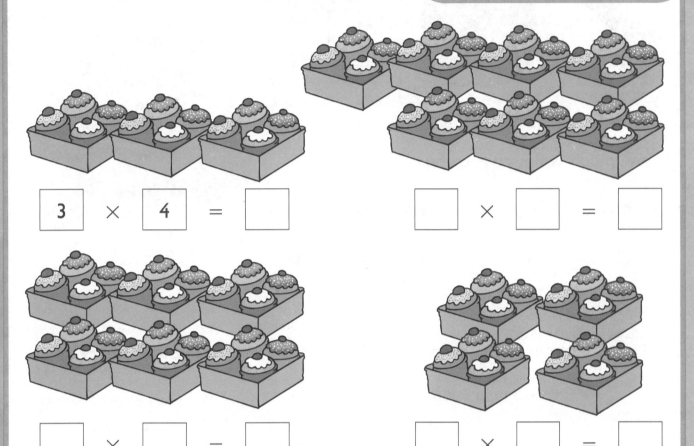

$$3 \times 4 = \boxed{}$$

$$\boxed{} \times \boxed{} = \boxed{}$$

$$\boxed{} \times \boxed{} = \boxed{}$$

$$\boxed{} \times \boxed{} = \boxed{}$$

2 Every number put into the number machine is multiplied by 4.

Write in the missing numbers.

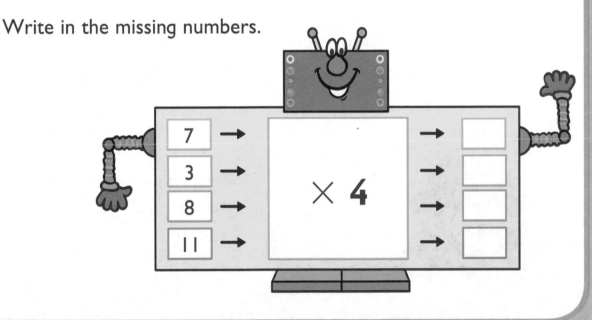

7 →

3 →

8 →

11 →

× 4

→

→

→

→

3 Here are some things for sale.

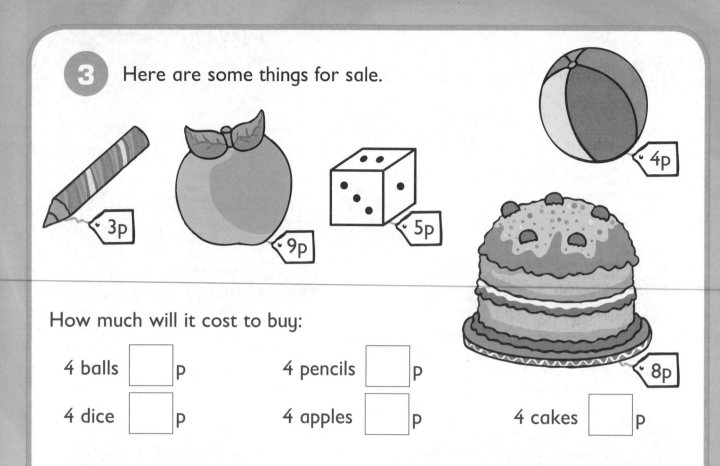

3p

9p

5p

4p

8p

How much will it cost to buy:

4 balls ☐ p

4 pencils ☐ p

4 dice ☐ p

4 apples ☐ p

4 cakes ☐ p

4 Colour all the shapes that have an answer to the four times table.

What do you see?

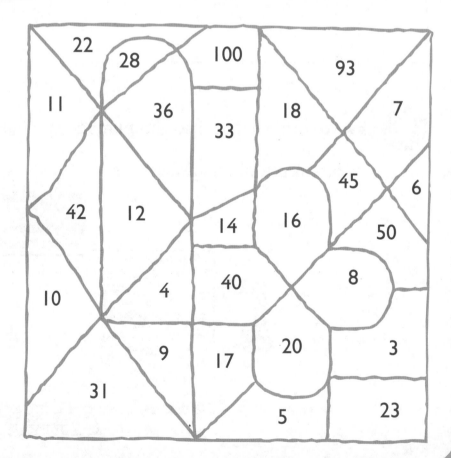

22 28 100 93

11 36 18 7

33

42 12 45 6

14 16 50

10 4 40 8

9 17 20 3

31 5 23

5 Here are the answers to the four times table.

Write in the missing numbers.

16 = ☐ × 4   28 = ☐ × 4

44 = ☐ × 4   20 = ☐ × 4

8 = ☐ × 4   40 = ☐ × 4

24 = ☐ × 4   4 = ☐ × 4

36 = ☐ × 4   48 = ☐ × 4

32 = ☐ × 4   12 = ☐ × 4

6 Some of the football players are wearing numbers which are answers to the four times table.

Circle the numbers.

Mixed tables

The number 12 is an answer to the three and four times tables!

$$\frac{3 \times 4}{4 \times 3} = 12$$

1   Count on in threes. Write the numbers on the orange snake.

Count on in fours. Write the numbers on the green snake.

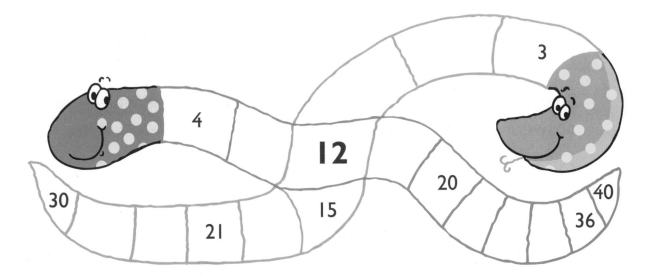

2   Draw a line to join each multiplication to its answer.

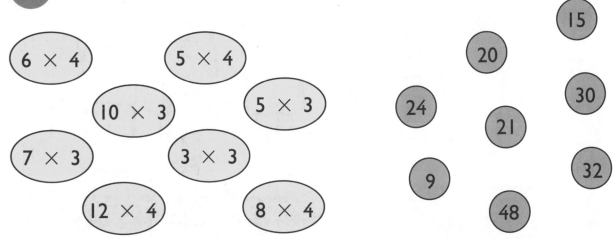

3 Here are some items for sale.

3p

4p

10p

5p

8p

How much will it cost to buy:

3 rolls [ ] p   4 biscuits [ ] p   4 muffins [ ] p

3 cakes [ ] p   4 crumpets [ ] p   3 biscuits [ ] p

How many biscuits could you buy for 18p? [ ]

How many crumpets could you buy for 24p? [ ]

4 Answer these questions.

What are six threes? [ ]   What is 2 times 4? [ ]

What is 6 multiplied by three? [ ]   Multiply 11 by 4. [ ]

How many threes in 12? [ ]   Divide 9 by 3. [ ]

Which number multiplied [ ]   How many fours
by 3 is 18?   in sixteen? [ ]

Mixed tables

1 Write the missing number on each machine.

2 Draw lines to join the multiplications which have the same answer.

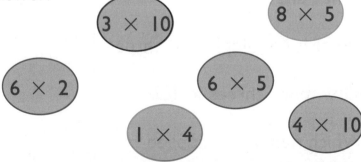

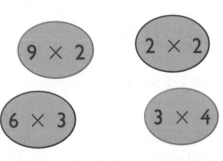

3 × 10   8 × 5

9 × 2   2 × 2

6 × 2   6 × 5

6 × 3   3 × 4   1 × 4   4 × 10

3 Look at these items.

Answer these questions.

How many sweets in 7 jars?   7 × | 10 | = | 70 |

How many socks in 5 pairs?   5 × | | = | |

How many bananas in 12 bunches?   12 × | | = | |

How many cakes in 8 boxes?   8 × | | = | |

How many crayons in 3 packs?   3 × | | = | |

I have 16 cakes. How many boxes is this? | |

I have 40 sweets. How many jars is this? | |

I have 12 socks. How many pairs is this? | |

I have 20 crayons. How many packs is this? | |

I have 15 bananas. How many bunches is this? | |

4 Here are some multiplications. Some are right and some are wrong.

Tick those which have the right answer. Cross those which have the wrong answer.

4	×	5	=	20	✓	8	×	5	=	40	
6	×	3	=	18		10	×	3	=	30	
5	×	10	=	55		9	×	10	=	90	
7	×	4	=	28		3	×	4	=	16	

5 Look at the numbers below.

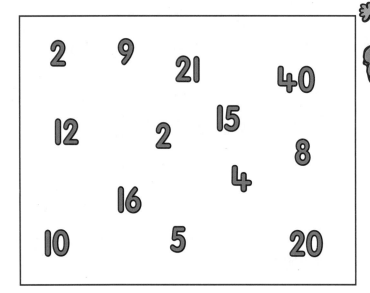

2   9   21   40
12   2   15
16   8
4
10   5   20

Circle any number which is in the two times table in blue.
Circle any number which is in the three times table in red.
Circle any number which is in the four times table in orange.
Circle any number which is in the five times table in green.
Circle any number which is in the ten times table in purple.

Have you noticed anything about these numbers?

6 Work out the answer to each multiplication. Then use the answer to find the correct colour in the code key.

Colour the picture.

Code key

10	=	dark blue
12	=	grey
20	=	green
30	=	yellow
40	=	light blue

7 Answer these questions.

What is 7 times 3? ☐

Multiply 6 by ten. ☐

Which number multiplied by 5 is 25? ☐

How many threes in 24? ☐

What are twelve fours? ☐

What is double 7? ☐

Halve 18. ☐

Divide 20 by 4. ☐

Answers

Two times table

Page 4

1, 2, 6, 4, 2, 12, 14, 2, 9, 10, 11, 24

Page 5

1   10, 2, 20, 14, 12, 22, 18, 24, 16, 8

2   8, 20, 14, 22

Page 6

3    $10 \times 2p = $ **20**p, $4 \times 2p = $ **8**p
      $6 \times 2p = $ **12**p, $8 \times 2p = $ **16**p

4   3 pairs and 6 socks, 5 pairs and
      10 socks, 9 pairs and 18 socks,
      7 pairs and 14 socks

Page 7

5   Join: $4 \times 2 \to 8$, $9 \times 2 \to 18$,
      $3 \times 2 \to 6$, $12 \times 2 \to 24$,
      $10 \times 2 \to 20$, $7 \times 2 \to 14$

6   4 – two dots on each dice
      6 – three dots on each dice
      8 – four dots on each dice
      10 – five dots on each dice
      12 – six dots on each dice

Ten times table

Page 8

1, 10, 30, 10, 50, 6, 10, 8, 90, 10, 11, 120

Page 9

1    $7 \times 10p = $ **70**p
      $10 \times 10p = $ **100**p
      $5 \times 10p = $ **50**p

2   Colour the shapes numbered:
      10, 20, 30, 40, 50, 60, 70, 80,
      90, 100
      It's a van!

Page 10

3   50p, 80p, 70p,
      110p, 90p

4    $6 \times 10 = 60$, $8 \times 10 = 80$,
      $4 \times 10 = 40$
      120, 9

Page 11

5   30, 70, 6, 9

6   Join the dots: 0–200 in the
      correct order. It's a turtle!

Five times table

Page 12

5, 10, 3, 20, 5, 5, 35, 40, 5, 10, 11, 5

Page 13

1    $30 = $ **6** $\times 5$, $5 = $ **1** $\times 5$,
      $20 = $ **4** $\times 5$, $50 = $ **10** $\times 5$,
      $35 = $ **7** $\times 5$, $10 = $ **2** $\times 5$,
      $15 = $ **3** $\times 5$, $25 = $ **5** $\times 5$,
      $60 = $ **12** $\times 5$

2    $3 \times 5p = $ **15**p, $4 \times 5p = $ **20**p,
      $6 \times 5p = $ **30**p
      Check that your child has drawn:
      $5 \times 5p$, $7 \times 5p$, $8 \times 5p$

Page 14

3   15, 25, 30, 40, 45, 55, 60, 65, 70, 75, 80,
      85, 90, 95

4   Colour fish: 5, 15, 45, 30, 35, 25

Page 15

5   Circle: 7×5, 10×5; 2×5, 11×5

6    $6 \times 5 = $ green, $4 \times 5 = $ red,
      $7 \times 5 = $ yellow, $3 \times 5 = $ blue,
      $9 \times 5 = $ purple, $10 \times 5 = $ orange

Mixed tables (twos, fives and tens)

Page 16

1   Double: 10, 16, 22, Halve: 3, 5, 8

Page 17

2    $10 \times 2p = $ **20**p, $4 \times 5p = $ **20**p,
      $2 \times 10p = $ **20**p

3    $5 \times 5 = $ yellow,
      $2 \times 5 = $ light green,
      $2 \times 9 = $ dark green,
      $4 \times 2 = $ light blue, $10 \times 2 = $ red,
      $4 \times 5 = $ red, $3 \times 5 = $ dark blue